FAMOUS PEOPLE
FAMOUS LIVES

Biographies of famous people to support the curriculum.

Guy Fawkes

by Harriet Castor

Illustrations by Peter Kent

This edition 2001

First published in 1998 by
Franklin Watts
338 Euston Road
London NW1 3BH

Franklin Watts Australia
Level 17/207 Kent Street
Sydney, NSW 2000

ISBN: 978 0 7496 4316 4

A CIP catalogue record for this book
is available from the British Library.

Dewey Decimal Classification Number: 941.06

Series editor: Sarah Ridley
Series designer: Kirstie Billingham
Consultant: Dr Anne Millard

Printed in China

Franklin Watts is a division of Hachette Children's Books,
an Hachette Livre UK company.

Guy Fawkes

When Elizabeth I was Queen
of England, a family lived in
York whose name was Fawkes.
There were three children –
two girls and a boy. The boy's
name was Guy.

At this time, people argued about the right way to worship God. One group was called Catholics, the other Protestants.

Queen Elizabeth was a Protestant. But she knew that some Catholics wanted a Catholic ruler instead. Parliament was afraid they would plot to kill the Queen, so laws were passed against Catholics. Many were fined or put in prison, and some were put to death.

Guy Fawkes' father was a Protestant. His mother was a Catholic. But when Guy was eight years old, his father died.

His mother got married again –
to another Catholic. Guy
became a Catholic too. For a
while he worked as a servant
for a Catholic lord.

Later, Guy became a soldier.
He was very good at the job.
Other soldiers noticed how brave,
and how religious he was.

Guy went abroad to fight for Spain, which was a Catholic country. He hoped that one day Spain would invade England and help put a Catholic ruler on the throne.

In 1603, Queen Elizabeth died. The new ruler was James VI of Scotland, who became James I of England and Wales too. He was a Protestant, but he said he would be kinder to the Catholics than Elizabeth had been.

However, James's Protestant
advisors thought this would be
too dangerous and, in the end,
James did not keep his word.
Many Catholics were very angry.

Some Catholics plotted to capture James and force him to change his mind. Some others wanted to kill him. They believed it was right to kill a bad king. But the plots failed.

People had tried to kill James several times before. No wonder he was often nervous!

Guy Fawkes was still abroad. But when he heard talk of a new plot against James, he came back to England to find out more.

The leader of this plot was Robert Catesby – Robin for short. He was good-looking and very charming. But his plan was a violent one.

King James was due to open
a new Parliament the next year,
1605.

Robin's idea was to blow up the House of Lords on that day, with gunpowder.

The King, his eldest son, the Queen and all the lords would be killed. Then there would be a rebellion and the Catholics would seize control.

Guy decided to join the plot.
There were five plotters at first.
They held a meeting at a
London inn and swore to keep
the plan a secret.

Later they needed extra help and money, so Robin Catesby persuaded more people to join. Eventually there were thirteen plotters.

A little house was rented by one plotter. It was right next to the House of Lords. At this time, the Houses of Parliament were mixed in with lots of other buildings, including shops and private houses.

You see – the House of Lords is just up there.

Guy Fawkes moved into the house and pretended to be a servant called John Johnson.

Now the plotters had to find a way to get the gunpowder under the House of Lords.

No one is sure exactly what they did next. Some people think they started digging a tunnel. It would have been hard work, and difficult to keep secret.

Other people say this story was made up.

Even if there *was* a tunnel, soon
the plotters must have stopped
digging. They had managed to
rent a storeroom near their little
house instead. This storeroom
was right underneath the
House of Lords!

Secretly the plotters took thirty-six barrels of gunpowder to the storeroom, and hid them under firewood.

Being a soldier, Guy knew a lot about gunpowder, so he was put in charge of it. When the time was right, he was going to light the fuse. Then, while the other plotters started the rebellion, he would escape abroad. He would explain to foreign Catholic rulers what had happened.

27

But one night, in another part of London, an unusual thing happened. A man called Lord Monteagle received a strange letter. It warned him to stay away from the Opening of Parliament.

Lord Monteagle took the letter straight to King James's most brilliant minister, whose name was Robert Cecil.

There are still arguments today about this letter. No one knows who wrote it, or why.

It might have been one of the plotters, who wanted the plot to be discovered.

Or it might even have been
Robert Cecil himself. He had
lots of spies. Perhaps he knew
about the plot already.

The handwriting is very strange.

Robert Cecil didn't show King James the letter straight away. If Robert already knew a little about the plot, maybe he wanted to wait so he could find out more.

My lord out of the loue I beare to some of youre frendes I haue a care for your preseruacion. therfor I would aduise you as you tender youre lyfe to deuyse some excuse to shift your attendance at thys Parliament for God and man hath concurred to punishe the wykydnesse of this tyme and think not slightly of this aduertisment but retyre yourselfe into the countrie where you may expect the euent in safety. For tho ther be no apparanse of any stir, yet I say thay shall receiue a terrible blow this parliament and yet not see who hurts them. This councel is not to be condemned becaus it maye do you good and can do you no harme for the dangere is passed as soon as you haue burnt the letter, and I hope God will giui you the grace to make good use of it. To whose holie protecciun I commend you.

To the right honorable
The Lord Mounteagle.

When he *did* show James the letter, Robert pretended he didn't understand it, so that James would think he'd solved the mystery himself!

On November 4th, 1605, the buildings near the House of Lords were searched. Around midnight, the searchers found the gunpowder hidden in the plotters' storeroom.

They also found a tall man
lurking nearby. He had boots
and spurs on, as if he was ready
to ride away at short notice.
It was Guy Fawkes.

Guy was questioned at first by the King himself.

Guy said he was John Johnson. He wouldn't give the names of any other plotters. He hoped they would have time to escape.

But when the others heard that Guy had been captured they didn't try to escape. They decided to start the rebellion.

Guy was taken to the Tower
of London.

To make him talk, he was
tortured horribly. Though he
had planned to kill so many
people, he believed he was right,
and he was very brave.

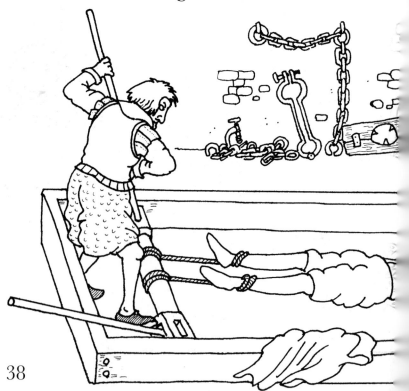

But eventually Guy admitted what his real name was, and began to talk about the plot.

Meanwhile, the other plotters were on the run. People hadn't joined their rebellion after all.

Several of them hid in a big house. There they had a dreadful accident. Some gunpowder had got wet in the rain, so they spread it before a fire to dry. There was an explosion.
One man was blinded.

We wanted to blow up the King, not ourselves.

At last the King's men arrived.
There was a shoot-out and
several plotters were killed,
including Robin Catesby.

The rest were captured and
taken to the Tower of London.
Two carved their names on the
walls of their cells. You can still
see the names today.

In January 1606, the remaining plotters were executed. One of them was Guy Fawkes.

Every year afterwards, bonfires
have been lit on November 5th
to celebrate the failure of the
Gunpowder Plot. And, even
though Guy Fawkes wasn't the
plot's leader, November 5th is still
often called 'Guy Fawkes Night'.

Further Facts

Is this story true?

There are many uncertainties about the Gunpowder Plot, because we don't know whether people at the time were telling the truth. Several plotters were tortured, so perhaps they were forced to say certain things. Others who gave information may have lied to protect themselves. Some people, for instance, think Robert Cecil set up the whole plot himself to make the King demand harsher laws against Catholics. We will probably never know for sure.

Still searching

Today, before every Opening of Parliament, the cellars of the House

of Lords are still searched in memory
of what happened in 1605.

A play about the plot?

William Shakespeare wrote a play
called 'Macbeth' soon after the
Gunpowder Plot was discovered.
It is about the murder of a Scottish
king, and is based on Scottish history.
But Shakespeare may also have
been inspired by the Gunpowder
Plot and other plots against King
James VI and I.

Some important dates in Guy Fawkes' lifetime

1570 Guy Fawkes is born, son of Edward and Edith Fawkes, in York, England.

1593 Guy Fawkes leaves England to become a soldier. He fights in Flanders for the Spanish, and later travels to Spain.

1604 A friend of Robert Catesby meets Guy in Flanders. He takes Guy back to England. Catesby tells Guy about the plot.

May, 1604 The five main plotters hold a meeting and swear an oath of secrecy.

March, 1605 The plotters rent a storeroom under the House of Lords.

October, 1605 Lord Monteagle receives a mysterious letter and takes it to Robert Cecil, the King's minister.

November 4th, 1605 The Houses of Parliament and surrounding buildings are searched. The gunpowder is found and Guy Fawkes is captured.

November 8th, 1605 Some plotters are found hiding at a house in Staffordshire. Several, including Robert Catesby, are killed.

January 31st, 1606 Guy Fawkes is executed in London. He is the last of the plotters to be killed.